P9-BYH-865

A Cache of Jewels

With

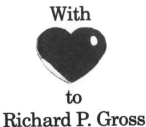

to
Richard P. Gross

No part of this publication may be reproduced in whole or in part,
or stored in a retrieval system, or transmitted in any form or by
any means, electronic, mechanical, photocopying, recording, or
otherwise, without written permission of the publisher. For
information regarding permission, write to Putnam Publishing Group,
200 Madison Avenue, New York, NY 10016.

ISBN 0-590-42586-2

Copyright © 1987 by Ruth Heller.

All rights reserved. Published by Scholastic Inc.,
730 Broadway, New York, NY 10003, by arrangement with
The Putnam Publishing Group.

12 11 10 9 8 7 6   1 2 3 4/9

Printed in the U.S.A.   23

First Scholastic printing, April 1989

A Cache of Jewels

and Other Collective Nouns

Written and illustrated by
RUTH HELLER

SCHOLASTIC INC.
New York Toronto London Auckland Sydney

A word that means a collection of things,
like a

CACHE

of jewels
for the crowns of kings…

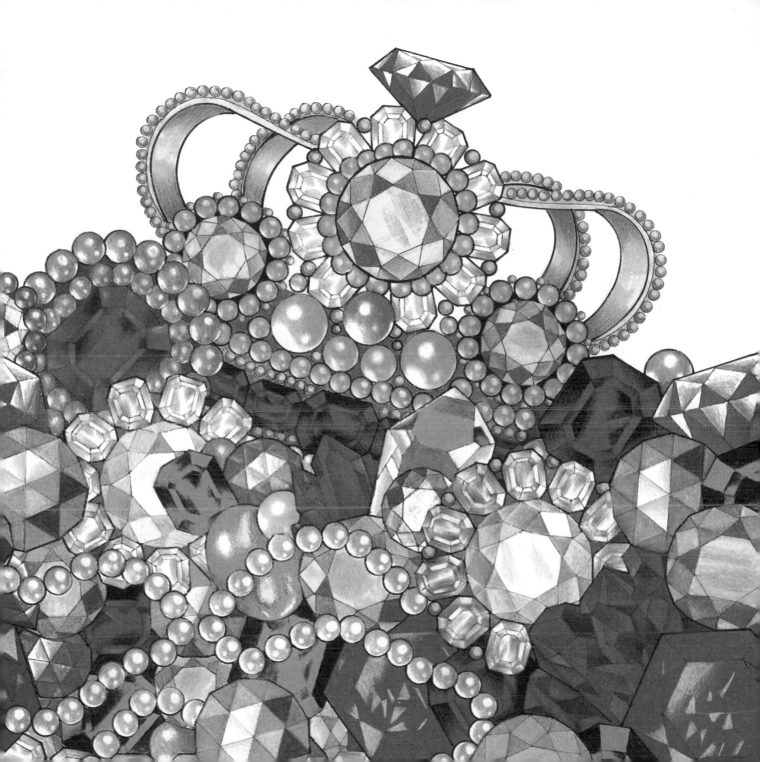

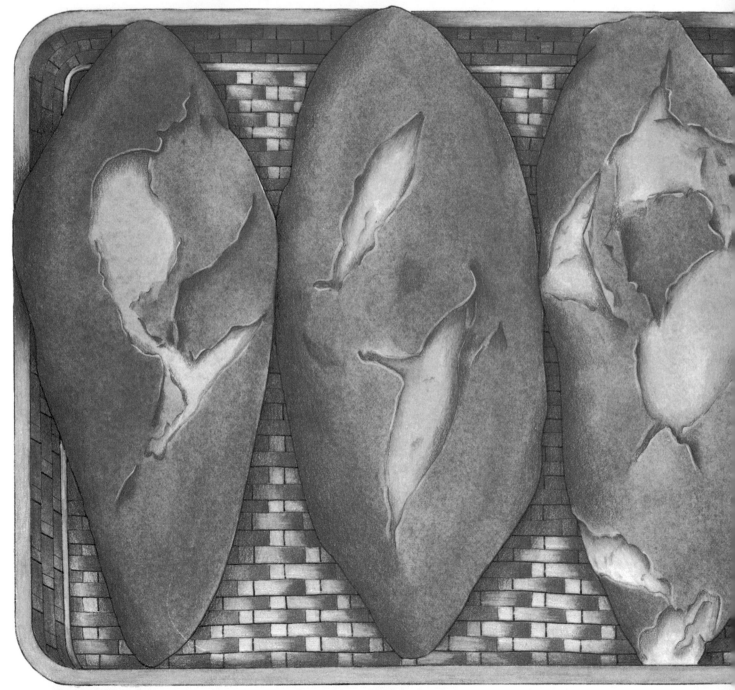

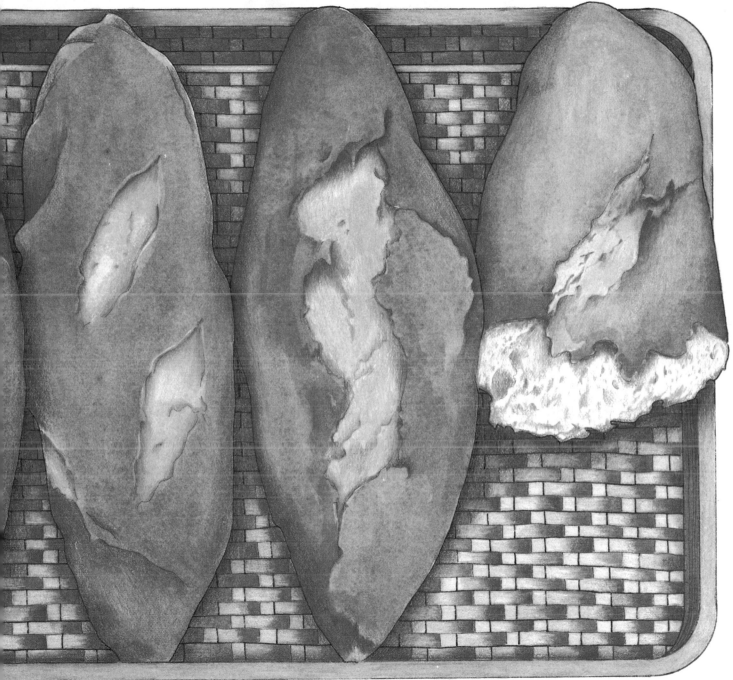

a **SCHOOL** of fish

a GAM of whales

a **FLEET** of ships
with
purple sails

a **BUNCH** of bananas

a
CLUSTER
of
grapes

a
BEVY
of
beauties

all different
shapes

a **MUSTER** of peacocks

a **FLOCK** of sheep

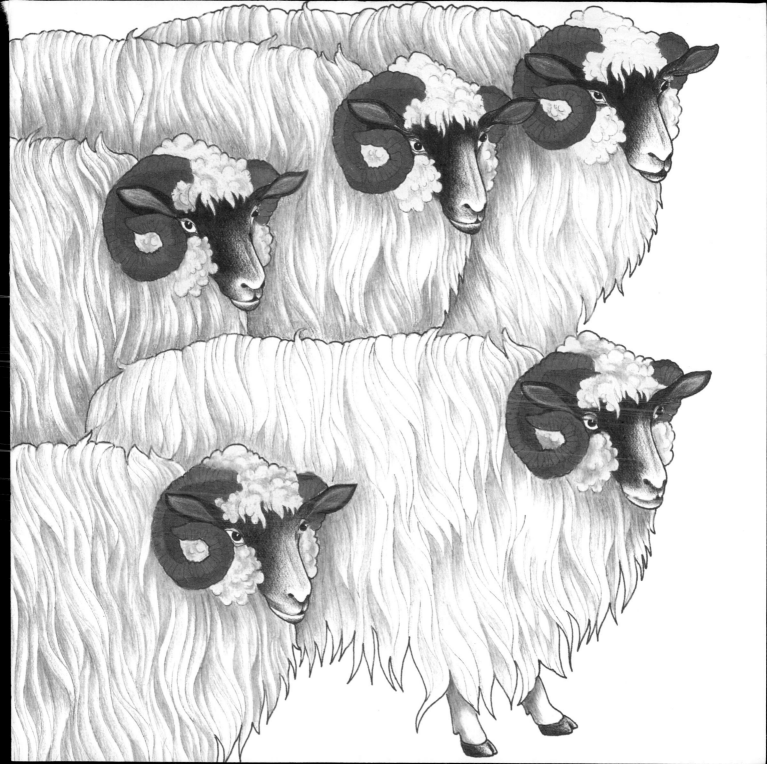

a
HOST
of
angels
fast
asleep

a **BOUQUET**
of flowers

a
SWARM
of
bees

a **KINDLE** of kittens
a
POD of peas

a **PARCEL** of
penguins

a
COVEN
of
witches
as
scary
as
these

a **DRIFT** of swans

a **CLUMP** of reeds

a
BED
of
oysters

a
STRING
of
beads

a
BROOD
of
chicks

a
CLUTCH
of
eggs

a
LITTER
of puppies on wobbly legs

a
PRIDE
of lions

a
LOCK
of hair

an
ARMY
of ants
from
here to…

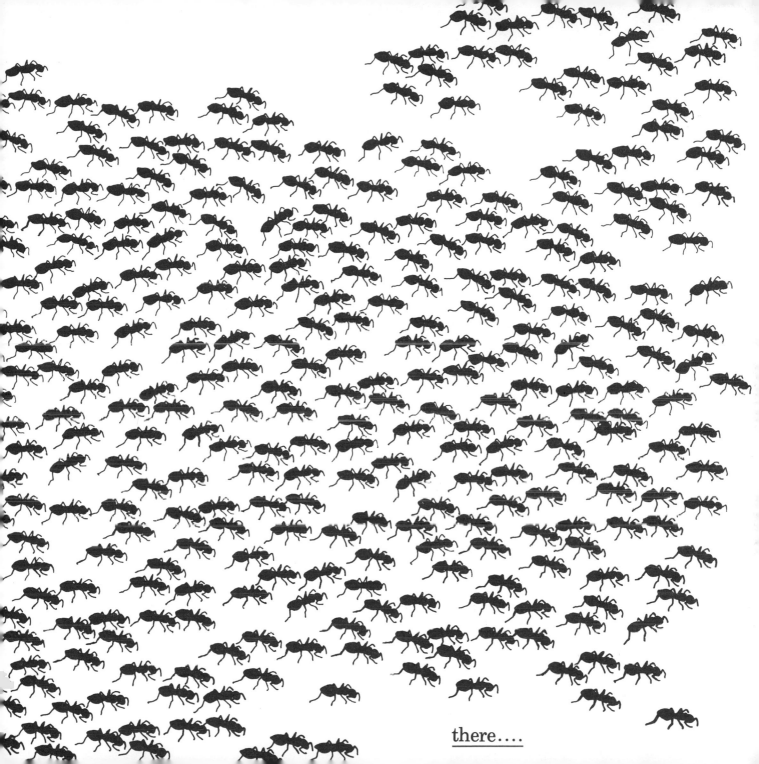

there....

About five hundred years ago
knights and ladies in the know
used only very special words
to describe their flocks or herds.

These words are used by us today,
but some were lost along the way,
and new ones have been added too.

I've included quite a few.

And there are more of these group terms
like **sleuth** of bears
or **clew** of worms
or **rafter** of turkeys
walk of snails
leap of leopards
covey of quails.

But nouns aren't all collective,
and if I'm to be effective,
I'll tell about the other nouns
and adjectives and verbs.

All of them are parts of speech.

What fun!
I'll write a book for each.

—*Ruth Heller*

<u>Note:</u> One collective noun can describe many groups, as in a **host** of angels, daffodils, monks, thoughts, or sparrows.

One group can be described by more than one collective noun as in a **gam** of whales, a **mob** of whales, a **pod** of whales, a **school** of whales, or a **run** of whales.